OUR NEW LIFE IN THE BIG CITY

by Guy Wakemore
illustrated by Ron Mahoney

Scott Foresman
is an imprint of

Glenview, Illinois • Boston, Massachusetts • Chandler, Arizona
Upper Saddle River, New Jersey

Every effort has been made to secure permission and provide appropriate credit for photographic material. The publisher deeply regrets any omission and pledges to correct errors called to its attention in subsequent editions.

Unless otherwise acknowledged, all photographs are the property of Scott Foresman, a division of Pearson Education.

Photo locators denoted as follows: Top (T), Center (C), Bottom (B), Left (L), Right (R), Background (Bkgd)

20 Horace Bristol/CORBIS

ISBN 13: 978-0-328-52691-8
ISBN 10:   0-328-52691-6

3 4 5 6 7 8 9 10 V0N4 13 12 11 10

Even as a child, Bill Straw dreamed of the huge cities of the North. He dreamed of the fine houses, trolley cars, and bright city lights.

Bill was born in 1908, in a small Georgia town called Appleseed, and like most of the surrounding communities, Appleseed was a rural community.

So, like most Appleseed residents, the Straws were farmers. They toiled in the fields every day, doing their best to raise crops on a small plot of land. They rented the land from a local property owner, but they never made much money. In fact, they barely made enough to survive.

The Straw family raised corn on the land, mostly. They had some peach trees and a vegetable garden, while they also cared for a few hogs, chickens, and goats. Their prize possession, however, was an aging dairy cow named Betsy Ross.

As a child, Bill spent half a day in school and the other half working on his parents' farm. His parents would have preferred that Bill go to school for the entire day, but they needed his help on the farm.

Reginald and Amelia Straw worked from sunrise to sunset, tending the crops and caring for their livestock. Yet something always came up that they didn't have time for—farm maintenance, usually. A wheel needed to be fixed on the plow, or a sick goat had to be cared for, or a new irrigation ditch had to be dug. Bill usually took care of these tasks. There wasn't much time in the day for leisure activities.

He didn't mind, really. Sure, Bill liked school. He was smart and relished most challenges. He loved figuring out math problems and studying ancient history. He also liked working on his parents' farm. It made him feel strong and grown-up.

He especially liked taking care of the farm animals. He had named each of them after a famous historical figure.

He had named their three hogs after his three favorite presidents: George Washington, Thomas Jefferson, and Abraham Lincoln. He'd named the two goats Napoleon and Josephine. He called their old, good-natured plow-horse Sir Thomas More.

Bill's parents were amused by the names he chose. "I declare," Reginald once told his wife, "we've got the most educated livestock in the whole of the South."

Although he liked farm life, Bill often daydreamed about bigger and better things. He dreamed about life in the big cities up North.

Bill had never been to a big city, but he'd heard stories about city life, and he'd read about it in books such as *David Copperfield,* which was set in England. That book made the city of London seem frightening and exciting at the same time. Bill figured there probably wasn't much difference between English and American cities. Everything he'd ever heard about big cities made Bill yearn to live in one.

In the city, trolley cars ferried you all around the city! Powerful trains came from and went to other parts of the country! Buildings were so tall you could lean out the window and get lost in the clouds!

At least that's how Bill imagined it. He'd never seen a tall building. The closest he'd come was when his father took him to the roof of their local church to repair the chimney, but the church was only two stories high.

In the cities, however, some of the buildings were hundreds of feet tall! Anyway, that's what Bill had heard—and he believed it.

So Bill was very excited to learn, one day in early 1918, that his family was planning to move to perhaps the greatest of all cities, New York City.

His parents didn't share his delight. They didn't consider cities to be glamorous or exciting. By 1918, however, life in Appleseed was becoming increasingly difficult.

Several seasons of drought had hurt the Straw family's crops. Even worse, many of their farm animals had caught some odd strain of the flu and were now either ill or dying.

The Straws might have overcome these burdens, but it almost didn't matter anymore. Reginald Straw was fed up with what he felt was unfair compensation for his work. He was tired of being a sharecropper, renting land from a white landowner. In exchange for all his work, he received only a small portion of the crops he brought in.

"Where would we go?" asked Amelia. She had never been farther from home than Bradley, which was only three towns away.

"Thinking 'bout New York," Reginald answered.

"New York?" said Amelia, stunned, as if he had said "Mars."

"There's a place called Harlem up there. Lots of people just like us. Black faces, good hearts. People who'd treat us right," Reginald said.

"I don't know, Reggie," said Amelia. Questions overwhelmed her. How would they get there? Could they find a place to live? How would Reggie make a living? Would they be able to find a school for Bill? "I have so many concerns about it."

"Of course you do, Amelia," said Reginald, with a smile. "It's only natural. But we're gonna sit down and talk about it. Work out the details."

"You really think it could work out?" asked Amelia, uncertainly.

"I think it's our only choice," said Reginald thoughtfully. "Lots of folks like us are moving north now. More every day. They say there are plenty of opportunities up there. It's the only way to go."

"You mean it, Daddy?" Bill asked over and over. "We're going to New York?"

Reginald smiled at his son's enthusiasm at the news. "That's right, Bill."

"I'm gonna live in a city!" Bill shouted.

"Not just any city," Reginald added, proudly. "Greatest city in the whole country. Maybe the entire world—New York City!"

Soon, the family's long journey to New York began. They had to stop in many small towns along the way. In each town, Reginald would find temporary work as a laborer or a farm hand. Amelia made a little extra money by mending dresses.

After the Straws had earned a few dollars, they'd move on again. And so it went.

"Aren't we ever gonna get to New York City?" Bill asked his father one day.

"Of course we are," said Reginald. But in all honesty, he wasn't sure. New York City was beginning to seem like someplace out of a fairy tale, a distant, unreachable goal.

But the Straws were persistent. And after what felt like years (but was really only a few months), they arrived in New York City.

The borough of Manhattan was even more dazzling than Bill had imagined. Such tall buildings! Paved roads leading everywhere, and wide sidewalks to walk upon!

Bill had never seen so many shops before, either.

"There's so much to do," he told his parents. "How do people find enough time to do it all?"

His parents shrugged. They weren't thinking about New York City's attractions right now. They were thinking about more basic concerns: how to find an apartment, how to find work, and how to find a new school for their intelligent, talented son. These concerns needed to be addressed immediately, or the Straw family would be sleeping on the streets—cold, hungry, and miserable.

"First things first," said Reginald. "Gotta find a place to stay." And so, the family trudged uptown to Harlem, where they searched block after block, looking for a vacancy.

Eventually, they found a small apartment on the third floor of a walk-up building on 129th Street. It wasn't much to look at. The wallpaper was stained and peeling. The plumbing clanked, and the aroma of simmering cabbage filled the halls.

The apartment did have one thing going for it: It was cheap. In fact, Reginald was able to pay the first two month's rent outright with money he'd saved during the long trek from Georgia. At least they now had a roof over their heads. That was a major relief.

"So," he told his wife and son at the dinner table, that evening, "we've got a place."

"What now, Daddy?" Bill asked him.

"Next step," Reginald replied, "is for me to find some work, and that's exactly what I'm gonna do. Tomorrow, bright and early, I'm gonna go out and find a job." Reginald was as good as his word.

When he returned to the apartment the following evening, he brought two things with him. The first was a bag of groceries. The second was a welcome piece of news: He'd found a job.

Reginald had been hired by a large, prominent furniture warehouse located downtown. The owners needed a new night watchman and had decided that Reginald's qualifications fit the bill just fine.

"It isn't fancy work," he told his wife and son. "But it's a good, honest job. They gave me a uniform, a cap, even a flashlight."

"Do you get a gun, Daddy?" asked Bill, excited.

Reginald just laughed. "No, son," he said, chuckling. "No gun. But I do have a whistle. Wear it on a string around my neck. If I see anything suspicious, I'm supposed to blow on it, real loud."

"Sounds like a good job, Daddy," said Bill.

"Pays good too," Reginald grinned. "Problem is, it's a night job. Go to work at 11 at night and won't come home until 9 in the morning."

"That's a long shift!" said Amelia.

"It's what I have to do," said Reginald, sounding almost apologetic.

"But when will I get to see you?" Bill asked. "When can we play catch and stuff like that?"

"Oh, there'll be time to do all that," said Reginald, hastily. "I'm never going to allow a job to prevent me from spending time with my wife and son. . . . We'll do those things on the weekends."

"How 'bout me, Reggie?" Amelia asked quietly. "Should I be looking for work too?"

"No," said Reginald. "A night watchman makes good money here, 'Melia. More money than I ever made before, in fact. Sufficient for our needs."

"I don't know. Maybe I should find myself a job," said Amelia.

"Don't you worry about that, honey. Keeping house is work enough. Fact is, Bill needs one parent around during the week, doesn't he?"

"Okay then," said Amelia, smiling.

"Good," said Reginald, with a wide smile. "Now let's have some dinner. I'm starving!"

The next step was to find a school for Bill. The neighbor across the hall, George Green, had a son who was the same age as Bill.

"Sam goes to P.S. 112," George explained to Reginald and Amelia, the next afternoon. "P.S. stands for Public School, you understand?"

"Sure, sure," said Reginald, nodding.

"It's a good school, right here in Harlem," George explained. "Not like the ones I went to when I was a boy."

"Where'd you grow up?" asked Reginald.

"Way down South," said George, with a smile. "Little town called Sunshine, Florida."

"I've heard of it!" said Reginald, grinning. "Near the town of Lime Grove?"

"Not five miles away!" said George, slapping his knee. "How do you know Lime Grove?"

The two men spent the next hour remembering their youth in the rural South, swapping tales of friends and relations.

"Anyway," George said later, "Sam's in the fifth grade. Your boy's about the same level, most likely. Tomorrow, Amelia should go to the district office and register him, so he can get started."

"That's wonderful," said Reginald. "I know Bill can't wait to go back to school."

Bill *was* eager to go back to school. P.S. 112 was different, however, from any school that he had ever seen before.

In Georgia, he had gone to a one-room schoolhouse near his parents' farm. The new urban school in no way conformed to his idea of what a school should look like.

It was enormous—an imposing red brick building that looked like a palace. Not only that, but there were so many students! So many faces and bodies pushing through the halls, everybody talking and laughing and shouting at once.

"I'm scared," he told his mother on the first day of classes. "What if I get lost?"

"Just find a grown-up," said Amelia. "And tell him or her that you're new in school and you're lost. I'm sure any teacher will be happy to help a lost boy find his way."

"Okay," said Bill quietly. He couldn't remember the last time he'd felt so afraid.

Everything worked out just fine, however, thanks to Sam Green. A hefty, good-natured boy, Sam took an instant liking to Bill. Sam showed Bill how to find his way around the massive school building.

"Gee, thanks," Bill told Sam at the end of the first week. "I couldn't have navigated my way through this first week without you."

"That was nothing," said Sam, with a grin. "New boy needs to learn how to get around."

"Still, I appreciate it," said Bill.

"Hey, that's what friends are for," said Sam.

Bill adjusted to his new school quickly. It was more difficult, however, to adjust to the fact that he rarely saw his father.

Reginald worked long hours at the warehouse. When he got home in the morning, he would climb wordlessly into bed. After school, Bill had to be quiet because his father was still sleeping.

Bill and his dad had always been close. Back in Appleseed, they'd talked and worked together in the fields. In the evenings, they had even played games together. It was difficult getting used to this new setup. Bill found he missed his father—a lot.

"I miss spending time with Daddy," Bill confided to his mother one evening. They had just finished eating dinner. Amelia was washing the dishes, and Bill was doing his arithmetic homework. Reginald had left early that evening to run a few errands before his shift began.

Amelia gave her son a reassuring hug. "I know how you feel, honey," she said. "I miss your Daddy too, and I know he misses us. But you have to understand. It's tough to find work, especially for a black man. Your father is responsible. He makes sure we get food on the table and a place to live. He wants to make sure that you can go to school and grow up and become something other than a night watchman. You understand, honey?"

"I understand," said Bill, quietly. But he still missed his father.

"It's tough for me too, Bill," his father told him one Sunday while they were playing catch at a small neighborhood park. "Working all night. Never getting time with my family." The baseball sailed back and forth between them. "Someday, I'll get a better job," Reginald promised.

But Reginald never did find a better job. The years passed. He grew used to working at night. He was well liked among his co-workers. He gained seniority and got a raise. Amelia went to work too. She learned to type and got a job in an office. She enjoyed her new independence.

Meanwhile, Bill grew up. He graduated from high school and went on to college! Then came the day when Bill received his law degree. His parents were so proud. Their years of struggle and sacrifice had not been in vain.

One day, many years later, in 1948, Bill Straw returned to the old apartment on 129th Street. It was Thanksgiving, and he had come to visit his parents.

Bill lived in upstate New York now, where he had his own law practice. He didn't see his parents often, so he was looking forward to a wonderful reunion. His parents were much older, but they still looked beautiful to Bill. He hugged and kissed them both as he entered.

"Bill!" his father said, delighted to see him. "My son, the lawyer! Come in, come in!"

They sat him down at the kitchen table, where they all ate well—roast turkey, savory stuffing (Georgia-style), and tart cranberry sauce.

"Delicious!" said Bill. "The best Thanksgiving dinner ever!"

After dinner, the lighthearted conversation turned a little more serious.

"Bill," Reginald said, clasping his son's hand. "I always tried to be a good father. But often," Reginald continued sadly, "I feel like I failed you. Working nights, always away, never around. . . ."

Bill shook his head dismissively. "Not true, Dad," he said. "I know you missed Mom and me. But you worked at that job, night after night, because you wanted a better life for us. You sacrificed so much for us. And I love you for that, Dad."

Reginald blinked away tears of joy. It seemed he hadn't failed his son, after all.

The Great Migration

In this story, the Straw family leaves the farm in Georgia and moves to New York in 1918.

Many African Americans who lived in the South moved to urban centers in the North in the early years of the twentieth century. This movement became known as the "Great Migration."

One of the key reasons for the Great Migration was jobs. During World War I, many men left the country to fight in Europe. This led to a shortage of manpower in the industrial North.

Northern factories needed workers. As a result, African American men could fill these job openings. They could make a better living working in the factories, than

they had been able to on farms in the rural South.

There were other reasons for African Americans to leave the South, including crop failures and lack of opportunities. Many parents moved their families so that their children would have better chances in life than they had experienced.

In all, more than 500,000 African Americans moved North during the Great Migration. People continued to move North after the end of the war too. Most historians say the Great Migration lasted from 1916 to 1929.